CONTEN'

THE FIRST STEPS
CHAPTER 1: FIRST TECHNICAL SKILLS

What you will need for this section:

- A set of lower-case tactile letter shapes
- A set of abc flashcards
- A clear and simple abc book

Getting started

Perhaps unsurprisingly, our course starts with a bit of homework for you. If you are to become your baby's first teacher, you need to pull yourself back up to speed on the basics of phonics – if indeed you ever learnt them in the first place. Educational methods have varied somewhat over the past few decades, and some of today's parents learnt to read in a virtually phonics-free environment. For this course, it is vital that you teach yourself to start thinking in the phonics-based *"a buh cuh"* rather than the more familiar *"ay bee see"*. Your first task is to make this second-nature.

The letter sounds are as follows:

Letter	Pronunciation	As in ...
a	a	**a**pple
b	buh	**bu**n
c	cuh	**cu**p
d	duh	**du**ck
e	e	**e**lephant
f	fuh	**fu**n
g	guh	**gu**n
h	huh	**ho**ney
i	i	**i**gloo
j	juh	**ju**st
k	kuh	**ka**rate
l	luh	**li**on
m	muh	**mu**mmy
n	nuh	**nu**t
o	o	**o**range
p	puh	**pu**ff
q	cwuh	**qu**een
r	ruh	**ru**n
s	suh	**su**n
t	tuh	**tu**sk
u	uh	**u**mbrella
v	vuh	**vu**lture
w	wuh	**wo**nder
x	cs	bo**x**

| y | yuh | **y**oung |
| z | zuh | **z**oo |

These letter sounds will need to be at the tips of your fingertips for the course, so take a short while over the next few days to practice spelling out words using the phonetic sounds.

You may have noticed that we make our letter sounds quite emphatic (with an *"uh"* at the end of many sounds). This is in contrast with what your child will be taught much later at school. School teachers (rightly) insist on a purer pronunciation of the phonic sounds. So, they will teach S as "sss" (as in "hi**ss**"), F as "fff" (as in "do**ff**"), N as "nnn" (as in ba**n**ana), and so on. Contrast this with our recommended "suh", "fuh" and "nuh" and you will see that the Baby Phonics Method pronunciation is significantly heavier. Why? Well, although the purer pronunciation gives a more accurate representation of the letter sounds, these sounds are not definite enough for a baby who certainly does not do subtlety. Over the next few months you will be attaching these sounds to different shapes, and they need to be clear and distinct.

What do I do?

The key theme of the First Steps stage is repetition. Your baby will need to see the link between the letter shapes and the letter sounds time and time again. Your job is not difficult, but it will require you to repeat and repeat and repeat. A warning: The Baby Phonics Method can only lead to success if you are prepared to keep covering the same ground until your baby is fully familiar with it.

Introducing the tactile abc letter set

A set of tactile lower-case abc letters is absolutely essential for the course and will form the core of the games you play with your baby in the first year. Tactile letters are simple, colourful letters in the shape of the letter they represent. Your baby can chew on them, finger them, push them up your nose and float them in the cat's milk bowl. If your baby has tactile letters around as his primary playthings he will soon become intimately familiar with the shape of each letter. If you name the letter sound every time you see him with it, he will also soon be linking shape with sound ... an easy way to learn basic phonics!

When choosing your lower-case tactile letters, clarity is key. Ideally, your letters should be:

- physically the shape of the letter they represent (rather than having the letter painted onto a jigsaw piece).

- a plain colour or colourless (rather than having distracting little pictures or patterns over each letter).
- robust and safe enough to withstand frequent games and chewing (be especially careful to avoid magnetic fridge letters; magnets can be very dangerous if swallowed).

Either a tub of bath letters or a jigsaw board should do the job well.

The first letter

Having found your tactile letters, you need to choose your baby's first letter. For these purposes, all letters are not equal. It is always nice to teach your baby the initial of his name, but certain letters must be avoided. Rotational letters are letters which have a different sound when rotated. "B" for example is "b" when it faces the right way, "q" when it is upside down, "d" when it's back to front, and "p" when it is both upside down and back to front. Other examples are "n" and "u". These letters will certainly confuse your child in the early stages. You'll start to say "Look, darling, here's your "b" ... oh, now it's a "p" ... well, OK, have it your way, it can be a "q" if you like ... no, "b" again". Your child will conclude that you're talking gibberish (and may well have a point). "M" is an excellent first choice, since it has none of these problems, and is easy to bang around and hold at the same time.

Once you have your first letter, you need to familiarise your child with it. Make sure his "m" (or other chosen letter) is always to hand. Babies will pick up and explore whatever is around them, and as soon as your child picks up his letter it's time to name it. It doesn't matter *what* you say, so long as you remember the two golden rules:

- **talk** about the letter whenever you see your child holding it; and
- **name** the letter sound every time you refer to it – *never* refer to it as "it".

Talk and name, talk and name. It doesn't get much more complicated than that at this stage, but it does need to be done over and over. This can't be emphasised enough. Your baby will not learn anything after a couple of showings. He *will* learn things which are a constant part of his environment, and so your job is just to keep on talking and naming his letter.

Suggestions for letter games

There are many ways you can incorporate tactile letters into the games you play with your baby. You will know what sort of games your baby enjoys most, and clearly your baby will respond best to letters if he finds them in the games he loves. However, in case you are stuck for ideas, here are a few suggestions:

- Cover up the letter with a blanket and play peepbo with it. "Where's "t"? Can *you* see "t"? Oh, *here's* "t". Shall we hide "t" again?"

- Hold your letter and make it dance towards your baby's face, ending with it kissing him on the nose. "M, m, m, m, *M* (kiss)". Just make sure that you are not moving it around so much that he can't see the shape of the letter.

- Hold up the letter and sing it to the tune of his favourite nursery rhyme. "W, w, w, w, w" might seem less inspiring to you than "Row, row, row your boat", but it's unlikely your child will have such fine feelings.

None of these games is rocket science, and you will think up plenty of your own (there are more suggestions in the **Suggested Activities** chapter on page 24). Just as long as your baby is having fun and you are linking the letter sound with the letter shape you are doing the right thing.

After a few months of playing with and talking about your first letter, you will be able to ask your baby "Where's 'm'?" and see him select it from a range of objects. Congratulations! Your baby has learnt his first letter and is now ready to move onto his second.

The second letter ... and beyond

Again, when teaching the second letter you need to avoid the rotational letters. Once you have chosen your letter, teach it in exactly the same way as you taught the first, but don't put away the first letter or your baby will almost certainly forget it. Your baby should learn his second letter much more quickly and soon will be able to pick out either letter on request.

After your baby is familiar with two letters it will be time to bring out (and keep out!) your full tactile letter set. Now he will be of an age where he can pick and choose the letters he wants to play with, and he may surprise you by developing favourites. Although by this point there are more letters around, your job remains the same. Talk and name each letter that your baby picks up and keep on playing the letter games. If you let your baby set the pace you will find yourself naming letters on many occasions during the day, and your baby's learning will forge ahead correspondingly.

This is all there is to it. After a few months of this you can try asking your baby for any letter from the letter tray and (if he feels like co-operating!) he may be able to give it to you. At that point you *know* that he has mastered all of the basic phonic sounds. It's as simple as that.

Using abc flashcards

A well-designed pack of abc flashcards is a great investment at this stage. It is surprising but true that babies love flashcards. Because they are so simple, babies understand the concept of flashcards before almost anything else, and they find this remarkably exciting. Add to this the pleasure of a cuddle while the flashcards are being read and babies can become keen to do them again ... and again ... and again. Some parents find they need to hide them to retain their sanity! But they're great for laying down the foundations for good reading skills.

When choosing your abc flashcards, look for cards which:

- are very simple, showing the letter very clearly in a prominent position, with no more than one illustrative picture (if any). Ideally any picture will be on the reverse so that there is nothing to distract your child's attention away from the letter.
- do not use inappropriate examples to illustrate the letter sound. Classic errors here are "i" for "ice-cream", "u" for "uniform", "o" for "onion". Instead, look for examples which share the letter's sound, like "i" for "igloo", "o" for "orange", "u" for umbrella.

- do not make use of any other features (tactile spots, bright patterns) to distract your child away from looking at the letter itself.

We suggest that flashcards be used in a different but complementary way to the tactile letters. Whilst the tactile letters should be available for the baby to play with at any time of day, the flashcards should be kept out of reach and only brought down at time when you can put your baby on your lap and devote all your attention to him. Once you have your baby's attention, read through the flashcards in order for as long as your baby continues to show an interest. The flashcards display the letter on the front and an illustrative picture (ideally) on the reverse. Using both will help your baby to realise that letters are part of words. So, show him the front, saying simply "b", then flip the card and say "b – ball".

We suggest that you prevent your baby from grabbing and playing with the flashcards. Unlike the tactile letters, flashcards don't teach your baby the letter shapes through his sense of touch, and keeping them just out of his reach may keep his interest tantalised.

It will obviously be an advantage to do your baby's flashcards at a time when he is most receptive to absorbing new ideas. Many children (like many adults) are highly receptive at the start of the day, so after breakfast can be ideal. Try to read through the flashcards at least three times a day, but never force them on your child when he is not interested. Once your child's attention has wandered, there is no point at all in continuing, and you may even stifle his natural interest. Remind yourself that the point of the Baby Phonics Method is to follow your baby's own pace and then relax ... there will be plenty of other opportunities.

Using the abc book

A good abc book offers a third way to capture your baby's interest in letters through shared activities. Reading together is clearly a large part of beginning to learn to read, and before your baby becomes mobile, you have a captive audience.

When choosing your abc book, look for one which:

- displays the letter prominently and clearly. Your child will pay most attention to whatever is most dominant on the page, so ensure that it is the letter rather than the illustration which dominates.
- has only one letter on each page, if possible, to avoid confusion in your child's mind.
- has lower-case letters only; not lower and upper case together, and certainly not upper-case alone
- (as with the flashcards) avoids the "i is for ice-cream" problem.

Do be aware that many abc books are targeted at older children, who have very different needs. Older children can be stimulated by variety and a lot of detail on the page. Babies, on the other hand, need clarity. If you're saying "a" to a baby, and the same page also displays "b" and "c", plus lots of pictures, what is the chance of your baby actually looking at the "a" as you say it? And if he's not looking at it, he won't be linking the sound with the letter-shape. Your motto for the first year is: *the simpler the better.*

Once you have your abc book, keep it to hand and read through it with your baby as often as feels comfortable. Point to the letter as you read it and put a definite tone in your voice as you say the letter. There is no need to focus just on one or two letters here; start at the beginning and keep going for as long as the book holds your baby's attention. There is no point in continuing once his attention has wandered, but if he seems to be enjoying it, you can go back to the beginning and do it again and again. Babies enjoy familiarity and repetition, so the more you read the book, the more he is likely to want to hear it again.

Moving on to the rotational letters

Rotational letters provide one of the biggest challenge in teaching the basic phonic sounds, since the same letter shape has a totally different sound when it is turned around. There are two ways to deal with this.

Firstly, use the tactile letters consistently. If your "d" is a different colour from the "p", but otherwise is the same, then make sure you decide which is which and stick to it. If your baby has it upside-down, say, "Oh no! Your "d" is upside-down. Shall we put it the right way round? Look! "d"!" Making a game of putting it right can turn a difficulty into an opportunity.

Secondly, use the flashcards and ABC book to focus on the rotational letters. As these don't flip around so readily they will help your baby make the right associations and consolidate what he is learning through the tactile letters.

Do expect these letters to be some of the last your baby learns, though. Rotational letters are undeniably a complicated concept for a small mind to grasp.

Finally ... Some Dos and Don'ts

The Baby Phonics Method is designed to be simple and accessible to all parents. However, there are a few easy extra things that you can do to give your child the right environment in which to learn.

- **Don't** have the TV on in the background. You may feel that a small amount of designated "telly time" when your child actually watches the box is fine. But having the TV on whilst your child is trying to do something else will hinder his concentration. He will be trying to focus on his chosen task, but the bright lights and noises from the television will constantly draw his attention away. This won't help either of you when you are trying to teach him his letters.

You may also like to bear in mind that the American Academy of Pediatrics recommend that children under two should watch no television at all, and a study lead by the University of Washington discovered that babies who watched so-called educational videos were 17% slower in language development than babies who did not.

- **Don't** have too many toys with flashing lights and loud sounds. Babies find these irresistible (which is why they sell so well). But, they are setting your child's stimulation requirements far too high. If he is surrounded by these all the time, he will soon *need* something to be all singing and dancing before it can hold his attention. This will be a problem for the Baby Phonics Method; it will be even more of a problem when he starts school.

- **Do** make sure that you don't try to force your child if he isn't interested at that moment. Babies have moods like everyone else. If he is tired, hungry or simply not in the mood, trying to draw his attention to letters will only be counter-productive. All babies spend much of their time exploring their environment. Just make sure that it is in these times that you use the Baby Phonics Method.

Moving on

Once you are sure that your child is confident with the letter sounds of the whole alphabet, you are ready to focus wholly on the second stage. And pour yourself a drink ... your child has now reached a higher level of literacy than many children starting school. That's a great investment in his future.

THE FIRST STEPS
CHAPTER 2: FIRST LITERACY SKILLS

What you will need for this section:

- A selection of appealing baby books

What greater gift can we give a child than a love of books? A technical ability to read is clearly vital if a child is to succeed in life, but a genuine love of books can transform him. Through books, he can learn to empathise with others and experience feelings of wonder, sadness, fear and joy; enjoying relationships and situations that are entirely imaginary.

So how can we open up this wonderful world of reading for our children?

Below we have outlined three key phases in a child's development over the first year. For each, we have given suggestions as to how you can encourage books and storytelling with your child. The second and third of these are divided into two distinct sections: **shared time** and **independent time,** to reflect the different ways your child plays.

Birth to six months
Telling stories
From the moment that your child is born he will want to be held by you, look at you
and hear your voice. These are three of his ultimate comforts and telling him (not
reading) a story is one way of providing all of these. So, lay him down on your lap, hold his hands in yours and make eye-contact. Then, dredge up some fairy-tales from your memory, and re-tell them, making great use of expression and moving his hands with yours in illustrative gestures. Try to keep eye-contact with him as much as possible. When his gaze wanders, so does his attention, so that's your cue to vary the expression or pace of the story.

In this way, before your baby can even smile at you, he will hear an extensive vocabulary and modulations of language. Better still, he will begin to associate stories with fun and attention.

Reminders of some of the more popular fairy tales can be found in the **Suggested Activities** section on page 24.

Nursery rhymes

Nursery rhymes are full of life, language and music … and they require less concentration from you (perfect if you're feeling tired and low on inspiration). They help to root your child in his culture and have been used for countless generations to soothe children. Try to incorporate them into your child's life at every opportunity.

Books

Alongside this introduction to storytelling and nursery rhymes, it is, of course, important to introduce books. There is a huge variety of cloth books on the market: black and white for newborns and books full of colour for slightly older babies. Sharing these with your child will not only provide necessary stimulation, it will also show your child how books work. Children need to know which is the front and which is the back of a book; they need to learn to look at a book from left to right. They need to be able to turn pages and distinguish between text and pictures. These are skills that are picked up subliminally, and as you look at a book with your child you can start to model them to him.

Even at this young age you can encourage him to look for the picture. "Where's the elephant?" and physically put your child's hand on what you are describing. "*There's* the elephant!" Equally you can point out the text. "Look! This word says 'Mummy'", and (again) place your baby's hand on the word.

Approximately six to twelve months.
Independent time

It is a wonderful moment when your child can finally sit up. Suddenly a whole new world of opportunities opens before him. At last, he can make real choices and exercise a little independence. However, it is at just this point that it is easy (inadvertently) to allow books to disappear into the background. Bright and noisy toys make their appearance and, bit by bit, begin to take over.

Resist! If we want our children to be excited by books, we need to provide them with less obvious stimulation. We need to give them opportunity to choose from a range of attractive toys and books without lights that flash and sounds that blare. If you provide your child with a good selection of board and cloth books to chew and throw and shake and play with, he will soon learn that books are fun. Favourites will emerge and you will be able to see your child interacting with a book at his own level.

Shared time
When you are sharing books with your child, you can encourage him to turn the page with you and he will clumsily help you when he has got the idea. Half turn the page and tantalise him with what is to come. After a while he will push your hand (the page) away to see it more clearly.

As your child gets a little older and his manual dexterity improves he will be able to handle and enjoy lift-the-flap books. Once again you need to model how these books work. Initially help your child open the flaps and then, when his interest is aroused let him do it himself. He will soon discover the joy of looking at a book independently .

Your key objective when looking at books with babies this age is to demonstrate that *books are wonderful*. If you can hold your child's attention by reading the text exactly as it is printed, then do so, as this will help your child to realise that a word says the same thing every time it appears. But, if this isn't working .... don't worry. Talk about the book and have fun with it. It is your job to make the text come alive. Pretend to be the animal with sounds and actions e.g. snap snap (clap clap) crocodile, tickle tickle monkey. Engage your child fully. No one else is watching so you can be as silly and effusive as you like.

Approximately 9 months onwards
Independent time

This is the age when any pre-baby ideas of clutter-free space start to look like a distant dream. It is, however, possible to have some input into the form of clutter. If you can, try to create an environment which encourages your child to look at books in every room. It is vital to keep your child's books at his level. Books that are tucked away out of sight are doing no good. Try to keep piles of books in your living area, in the bathroom, at the nappy-changing area, in the kitchen. If books are accessible they **will** be looked at, no matter how active your baby is.

You can make your piles of books even more attractive by putting a baby chair or cushion on the floor next to the books. Then (hopefully!) you'll be able to watch as he proudly sits himself down to 'read' to himself. If you have modelled the whole experience of reading to him there will come a time when he will happily and confidently choose a book and be stimulated by a book, without any interaction from you.

Shared time

It is all too easy to be disheartened when your child gets to nine months or so and assume that all the input that you have given has been pointless. He doesn't seem to be interested in books at all. You sit down quietly with your child and attempt to read him a story – a beautifully illustrated story with eye catching pictures, full of the most wonderful language and rhyming text. Yet after only a moment he either pushes the book away or tries to eat it. But don't despair. At this time many children have discovered the delights of crawling and suddenly any sedentary activity completely loses its appeal. You just have to pick your moments carefully. Maybe a story at cuddle time will convince your baby that this book is really worth his attention. Maybe not ... in which case you can do no more than to make sure that books are around and available. He'll be back, once he's firmly mastered the skill of crawling.

If you find yourself in this situation, don't forget the importance of storytelling. You can bring your child's new drive for activity into the story, zooming around the room pretending to be the Big Bad Wolf, or pulling up together the Enormous Turnip.

Dos and Don'ts

- **Do** tell stories from the word go, taking advantage of your baby's inactivity and love of one-to-one time.

- **Do** introduce books early on so that they are quickly familiar and friendly objects.

- **Do** share books regularly with your child, making him aware of both the text and pictures.

- **Don't** surround your child with too many 'over stimulating' toys (including some books) that have flashing lights and make loud noises so that books with words appear boring in comparison.

- **Do** keep your babies books accessible so that he can read them whenever he fancies.

- **Don't** become too precious about books. They are there to be looked at and if a few get damaged along the way, it is for a good cause.

- **Do** do your best to make every book exciting and wonderful!

  And finally ...

- **Don't** have the TV on while you're reading stories.

THE FIRST STEPS

CHAPTER 3: SUGGESTED ACTIVITIES

Below you will find suggestions for activities to help you put the Baby Phonics Method ideas into practice. Do note your baby's responses and let us know the results!

Technical strand

Make sure that your tactile letters are always around and accessible.

To start off, choose just one letter to be your baby's first letter. Make sure your baby has it to play with as much as possible. Include talk about the letter-sound in your normal patter of baby-talk. So ... "here's your **g** again. What *are* you doing with that **g**? Whoops, you've dropped **g**. Have **g** back again"

Try to incorporate this into your day-to-day life, so that without thinking about it you are naming letters several times a day.

Play (necessarily basic) games with the tactile letters, such as:

- cover the letter with your hand and then remove, saying "Where's **s**? Peekabo!"
- make the letter kiss different parts of your child's body, talking about it all the time. "a, a, a, a, a, **A**! (kiss)"
- sing the sound of the letter your child is holding (or you are showing to your child) to any nursery-rhyme tune
- any other game which works for you, so long as the baby can **see** the letter and **hear** the letter-sound

Is it bath time? Then choose a "**b**" to take upstairs with you.

Are you going for a walk? Maybe you should put the "**w**" by the hamster cage so he knows where you've gone.

Is Daddy going to work? Perhaps he should take the "**d**" with him ... and bring it back at the end of the day.

When you think your baby is becoming familiar with his first letter, hold up two letters and ask him to find the one he knows.

Point to note: It's important never to let him guess. If he doesn't seem to know, tell him immediately. Otherwise, he will start to remember his (wrong) guesses rather than your (correct) teaching.

Sit your baby on your lap and read through the letter flashcards with him. First read the letter, then turn the card over and read the illustrating word. Keep on going for as long as it holds your baby's attention, however short a time this may be.

If your baby tends to lose interest before you get to the end of the alphabet, just cut down your flashcard pile and concentrate on a few letters for a while. You can add in the other letters later.

Your baby will almost certainly want to reach out and grab the flashcards. Possibly, keeping them out of his reach will keep his attention directed on the cards. If not, then let him play with them. You will find for yourself which works best.

Try to look at the flashcards every day, if possible.

Read through the **abc book** with your baby as often as you can. But only ever keep reading for as long as you have your baby's attention.

Keep your baby's books and tactile letters out and accessible as much as possible. Books and letters should be the first and most accessible playthings.

Help your baby to develop an ear for the initial sounds of words. Whenever you can, repeat the initial letter of the word before saying it. So, try saying something like:

"Molly's found a monster in her book. I hope he doesn't m, m, m, m, m, m, m, m, **MUNCH** her!" (as you pretend to gobble your baby); or

"Jamie's a p, p, p, p, **PICKLE** who needs a t, t, t, t, **TICKLE**!"

The more you can do this, the easier it will be for your baby to recognise the component sounds of words ... an essential skill for reading and spelling.

Literacy strand

At any quiet moment in the day, retell traditional fairy-tales to your child, such as:

- The Three Little Pigs
- Little Red Riding Hood
- Cinderella
- Jack and the Beanstalk
- The Enormous Turnip

Ian Beck has written and illustrated a nice range of tales if you need to familiarise yourself with the stories. Wikipedia, of course, has an extremely exhaustive list.

Share books with your baby, drawing attention to both the pictures and the print. Use his hands as a pointer, asking and answering questions with him.

"**Where's** the elephant?" "**There** it is."

Provide your child with a selection of attractive, colourful books that are easily accessible to him.

When reading with your child, encourage him to turn the page himself (or turn it with his hand in yours)

Share a wide selection of lift the flap books and encourage your child to discover what is behind the flap himself. It helps if there is a repetitive text and **meaningful flaps**, so that what is revealed actually adds to the story.

Two good examples of this are *"Dear Zoo"* and *"Oh Dear!"*, both by Rod Campbell.

Choose a book with pictures of animals. As you are looking at the animal, make the animal noise or make an action to represent that animal – e.g **SNAP SNAP** crocodile or **TICKLE TICKLE** monkey.

THE FIRST STEPS
CHAPTER 4: PRODUCT RECOMMENDATIONS

So, you're in the children's section. You're faced with a huge selection of toys and books, each competing with each other to catch your (not, at this age, your baby's) attention and tempt the money out of your purse. Which should you consider? Which will genuinely help and capture the attention of your baby, and which will gather dust in the corner?

The idea behind these product recommendation sections is to give you some pointers on how to apply the principles of the Baby Phonics Method when choosing books or toys for your child. We are most certainly *not* trying to dictate to you or to tell you what to buy. What we do hope to do is to show you how it is possible to extend the Baby Phonics Method ideas to the products you choose to have in your home. When it seems appropriate, we have included details of specific products, but more importantly we aim to offer guidelines to the mindset of the Baby Phonics Method.

We have given separate recommendations for each of the two Baby Phonics Method strands. Naturally, the advice in each section is very different and it is important to remember that *both* strands play a part in your baby's development. Most products will tend towards one strand or another; but few will fully fit the recommendations for both. The ideal is to have a good mix available for your baby so that each strand can be developed without effort.

TECHNICAL STRAND

When choosing books for your baby at this early stage, the key requirement is **clarity**. Bear in mind that your baby's technical learning is currently centring around learning the sounds of individual letters and words. To help him with this, a book needs to have the letter (or word) clearly displayed, away from other distracting detail, and ideally with a compelling picture to illustrate it. Your baby can easily be swamped by too much stimulation on a page.

Abc books

It can be surprisingly hard to find books which meet all the criteria outlined in Chapter 1. If the book you find falls down on one or more aspects, try to be aware of its defects and do your best to correct for them.

We have found the following books to be useful:

- ABC Flip Flash Pad, published by Autumn Publishing

- **Early Learning: ABC (Ladybird Minis)**
- Topsy and Tim's Little ABC Library, published by Ladybird
- Most of the Ladybird ABC books from the 60s and 70s

Some of these are clearly out of print, but are available second hand from Amazon and are well worth snapping up.

First word books

There are many books in the bookshops claiming to be first word books for babies. However, books which have between ten and a hundred words on a double page spread will overload your baby with information and are not appropriate for this stage. Look for books which will help to make your baby **print aware**. In other words, to bring him to realise that the print on a page *speaks* to you and can speak to him.

If your baby is going to learn to recognise a word in a book, then that word should ideally be set out:

- in a large, clear font;
- in a straight line;
- in lower-case letters; and
- separate from other words and detail on the page.

We recommend the following:

- Most books from the **Bow-Wow** series by Mark Newgarden and Megan Montague Cash, especially **Bow-Wow Orders Lunch**. (Be aware that a few books in this series have no words at all)

- **Words**, **Toys**, or **Animals** first word books, illustrated by Gaynor Berry
- Old-fashioned **picture books**.

Unfortunately, many of the best first word books are now out of print. Again, it is often worth looking on-line or in charity shops for these, especially ones published by Ladybird in the 1970s.

LITERACY STRAND

In contrast to the technical section, there is a host of excellent books on the market that you could buy to cover the literacy strand. Here we have recommended many classics, but we have grouped them into particular categories to help you choose a range of texts to meet all your baby's needs.

Lift-the-flap books

These books are perfect when your child can sit up and help you to open flaps, turn pages and really interact with you. Equally, they are ideal for when they become a little more independent and can 'read' to themselves. Look for lift the flap books that actually have flaps that add to the story, where vital information is hidden and the flap needs to be opened for it to be revealed.

- **Dear Zoo** Rod Campbell
- **Where's Spot?** Eric Hill
- **Peekaboo Farm!** Emily Bolam

Sensory texts

There are many books on the market that encourage your baby to **feel** as well as look. Choose books that develop your baby's vocabulary, where what is felt is also described.

- Any book from the **Usborne touchy-feely books** series. Eg **That's not my reindeer**
- Any book from the **Ladybird Baby Touch series.** Eg **Colours**

Board books and rhyming text

Look for board books that contain simple rhyming text, few pages and clear illustrations. Your baby will love to turn the pages himself and enjoy the illustrations.

- Any book from the **Poppy Cat** range by Lara Jones
- **Tickle Tickle** Helen Oxenbury
- **Dinosaur Roar** Paul and Henrietta Stickland

Repetitive texts

There are so many classic children's books that contain simple repetitive text. As children grow, repetition encourages them to join in and play their part in the book sharing.

- **The Very Lonely Firefly** Eric Carle
- **The Very Quiet Cricket** Eric Carle
- **The Very Hungry Caterpillar** Eric Carle
- **We're Going On a Bear Hunt** Michael Rosen Helen Oxenbury

Books to encourage songs and rhymes

These books are fun to read aloud and encourage you to sing and play with your child.

- **Head, Shoulders, Knees and Toes...** Illustrated by Annie Kubler
- **Row Your Boat** Rhyme by Pippa Goodhart
- **Old Macdonald had a Farm** Illustrated by Pam Adams

Longer texts for quiet moments

Look for texts that scan well, that are full of rhythm, rhyme and wonderful words. They will help your child begin to understand how language works. If your child is very active and finds it hard to listen, choose a quiet time before a nap or bedtime when they can relax into you and listen.

- **Rumble in the Jungle** Giles Andrae David Wojtowycz
- **Each Peach Pear Plum** Alan and Janet Ahlberg

This is the end of the *First Steps* section.

Once you have read these chapters, we highly recommend you contact one of our consultants for a half hour phone conversation. We will answer any questions you may have and work with you to tailor the Baby Phonics Method to your particular circumstances and your child.

Phone calls call be booked through our website www.babyphonicsmethod.com and cost £30 for a half hour call.

We hope to speak to you soon!

the
babyphonics
method

INTRODUCING NUMBERS

from 6 months onwards

INTRODUCING NUMBERS
CHAPTER 5: BEGINNING NUMERACY

What you will need for this section:

- A 0-20 number-line
- A 1-100 number-chart

At around the time your baby is six months old, we suggest you introduce your baby to a number-line.

What is a number-line?

A number-line is a series of number flashcards from zero to twenty, designed to be displayed in sequence. The aim is to help your child to develop a corresponding mental number-line which he can call to mind (and later use for number manipulation) whenever numbers are mentioned.

When choosing your number-line, look for flashcards which:

- are clear and simple; just the number on a plain background with no illustration.
- can be displayed in a highly visible location in your house.

If you are having any difficulty finding a suitable number-line, it is easy to make and laminate the cards yourself. A Baby Phonics Method consultant will happily email you a proforma set of cards for printing and laminating.

Why use a number-line?

As with letters, the first year is the best time for your baby to start to link the number sounds with the number shapes.

It is important to realise, however, that numbers are conceptually different from letters. Letters can be learnt in any order and jumbling them up is the way we use them to make words. Numbers, on the other hand, live in a **sequence**, and it is as important to learn this sequence as to recognise the number itself. This is why we base our number teaching around the number-line rather than on loose number sets.

How do I display the number-line?

The number-line should be put up in one long line (or two lines if one is impractical). Try to ensure:

- that there is a small gap between each number so that your baby only focuses on one number at a time;
- that nothing else that your baby might find exciting or distracting (such as photographs or pictures by an older child) is displayed in the same area; and
- that if at all possible the number-line is displayed where you can point to it as you feed your baby.

Why now?

Crucially, you will have started to wean your baby by (or even before) this age. If his muscles are strong, he may already be able to sit up in a high chair; if not, he will do so soon.

Meal times provide you with a great opportunity to introduce your baby to numbers. If you have displayed your number-line in the area where you are feeding your baby, you have an opportunity to bring numbers into social time with a captive audience ... a perfect learning environment.

What do I do?
Learning the numbers

Without a doubt, at the start you will need to employ all your talents and parenting skills to transfer the orange gloop from spoon to firmly clamped mouth. However, once your baby begins to co-operate, you'll be able to relax a little more at mealtimes and start enjoying the interaction with your baby. So, try using the number-line as part of the in-meal entertainment. Number songs are generally the best way to start. Take "Ten green bottles" for example. As you sing "Ten ...", you point to the number 10 on the number-line. Then carry on with the rest of the verse, doing whatever actions or embellishments come naturally. When you reach the word "Nine ...", point to the number 9. And so on.

In the *Suggested Activities* chapter, we have included suggestions for other number songs. There are so many around that you can't fail to find some you both like.

It's not particularly challenging; it doesn't demand a degree in maths. But it does mean that your baby will be having fun at mealtimes and at the same time learning to link the number names to their written equivalents.

The second way of introducing your baby to the number-line is simply to stand in front of it with your baby in your arms. Babies being babies, he will probably reach out and try to touch the cards. Don't let him pull them off the wall, but do let him get close enough to point to a card. Then, as he does, name the number he's pointing to. Continue this for as long, and as often, as he wants to point, and it will significantly help him to start recognising the numbers.

Learning to count

Of course, simply recognising a written number isn't the same as being able to count. Numbers are there to be **used**, and you can count with your baby whenever an opportunity presents itself. Try some of the following:

- Make it a rule never to go up and down stairs with your baby without counting each step. This can become second nature to the extent that you find yourself counting steps with the cat and the washing as well. But if it's becoming second-nature to you, it's also becoming second-nature to your baby ... and that's an achievement.

- Always count your baby into fun activities. So, when you've put him in a swing or you're holding him on the top of a slide, don't say "Ready, steady, go!"; say "One ... two ... three ...WHEE!". It all helps to get the structure of numbers established in your baby's mind.

- Count your baby's bricks with him when you're building a tower or stacking cups together. "One, two, three, four ... oh, they all fell down.

Let's try again". By far the most effective way of showing your baby how to count is to **move** each object as you count it. This shows your baby that the number sequence is not just another nursery rhyme, but emphasises that each number refers to a different brick.

- You can do a lot at mealtimes, especially with the number-line nearby. Cut your child's banana into ten pieces and count them with him. Then point to the 10 on the number-line and say "But if Johnnie were to eat one ..." and show him how your finger jumps from 10 to 9 as one disappears from his plate. You can then help him count up the pieces of banana left, point to 9 on the number-line and go through the process again. If this holds your child's attention, it's a fantastic exposure to the basic manipulation of numbers.

- We always found that we relied heavily on the microwave for heating up baby food. And often, you only need a few seconds. So, instead of relying on the microwave's timer, count the seconds out loud, pointing to each number on the number-line as you do so.

- As your baby gets a little older, he may like to play with the buttons on the cooker's timer (assuming, of course, it's away from the hot oven). You can use the number-line to show him that when you've put 20 minutes on the timer, the 20 matches the 20 on the number-line. Then you can check it again in one minute and it's gone down to 19 ... and, look, if you go down one on the number-line you get to 19 as well. The joy of being able to play with the buttons, combined with the interest in the concept means that some children can keep going with this game for ten minutes or so.

As with the letters, it's over to you to be creative with the number games. You know best what holds your baby's attention. If you're counting with your baby and talking to him about the number-line you're doing it right

... and laying the foundations for solid numeracy skills later in life.

Moving on

When your baby is eighteen months, we suggest displaying a number-chart with numbers 1 – 100. It is clearly impractical to have a number-line which runs to 100, but a number-chart is the next best thing and is a good way of introducing your child to numbers above 20. We suggest displaying it somewhere where your child can reach it and point to it. Every time he points to a number, **name** it. It will also help if you can **count** through the numbers with your child from time to time, pointing to them as you do so. However, by eighteen months, your child may not want to stay around for this. Don't worry. Just keep the number-chart on display and react whenever your child points to a number.

Finally, remember to number-spot with your child when you're out and about. House numbers are a great resource for this age-group. As you walk with your child on a Sunday afternoon stroll, point out the house numbers on the houses you pass. If you can capture your child's interest in this game, he'll soon start to understand the way that two (or even three) digit numbers work together.

From this point on, your child's numeracy development will find its own expression and momentum and you will know best how to take your child forward. Keep the number-line up, be creative ... and let us know how you get on!

CHAPTER 6: SUGGESTED ACTIVITIES

Sing number songs to your baby during mealtimes and point to the numbers as you do so. Some popular number songs are:

- 10 green bottles
- One man went to mow
- 5 little ducks went swimming one day
- 5 current buns in a baker's shop
- 5 little men in a flying saucer
- 5 little speckled frogs
- One elephant came out to play
- 1, 2, 3, 4, 5 Once I caught a fish alive

If these are holding your baby's attention, then expand the songs for numbers all the way up to 20.

Let your baby explore the number-line in your arms. Let him reach out and touch any number he chooses, and then read the number he has touched. Then move his finger along so that you read them all in order (or until he loses attention).

Count the stairs out loud when you are climbing them with your baby.

Count the pieces of food your baby has on his plate and show him the corresponding number on the number-line. Then, show him how your finger jumps down one on the number-line when he has eaten one, and help him count the pieces up again.

If you are counting seconds on the microwave, point to the numbers on the number-line as you do so.

Look for numbers out and about, and point them out to your baby. Speed limit signs are very clear and when your child is a little older spotting them can become a game. Supermarkets often number their aisles with prominent numbers and if you draw your child's attention to these they may be a welcome distraction during your weekly shop.

Point out house numbers to your baby when you're on a walk.

Play hide-and-seek with your baby, and count to ten out loud.

In general, use any excuse you can to count things with your baby, remembering (where possible) to move each item as you count it.

INTRODUCING NUMBERS
CHAPTER 7: PRODUCT RECOMMENDATIONS

There are a number of products on the market aiming to familiarise children with numbers, and fortunately, many of them are excellent.

The First Year
123 books

During the early stages, once again the key feature to look for is clarity. Ask whether the **number itself** is given sufficient prominence, ideally:

- in large print;
- with the number ("5") given more prominence than the word ("five"); and
- separate from the illustration.

We recommend **Numbers** illustrated by Gaynor Berry.

Counting toys

Developing numeracy is about more than recognising numbers, and it is worth investing in some games which support your child's growing **ability to count**.

We recommend:

- Children's abacuses, or any toy which has (safe) moving parts to be slid forward and backwards along an enclosed strut.
- Loose toys, such as soft bricks or chunky building blocks.

The Second Year
Number sequence toys

During this year you will focus less on simple number recognition and more on learning the number sequence.

We recommend:

- A number jigsaw puzzle where the shaped numbers fit into pre-shaped holes;
- Plain number cubes with one number on each which can be set out in order. Try to avoid cubes which attempt to combine letters and numbers, or interlace the number with detailed pictures.

For All Ages

Singing number songs is an invaluable way of sharing numbers together, and can bring together number recognition, counting and the number sequence.

We recommend the following websites for ideas:

- http://www.bbc.co.uk/dna/h2g2/A3577647
- http://www.bigeyedowl.co.uk/show_songs.php?t=7
- http://bussongs.com/counting_songs.php

This is the end of the *Introducing Numbers* section.

Once you have read these chapters, we highly recommend you contact one of our consultants for a half hour phone conversation.

Not in the UK? Not a problem. We are used to holding consultations over Skype.

Phone calls call be booked through our website www.babyphonicsmethod.com and cost £30 for a half hour call.

We hope to speak to you soon!

the
baby phonics
method

MAKING PROGRESS

from approximately 12 months onwards

CHAPTER 8: DEVELOPING TECHNICAL SKILLS

What you will need for this section:

- A way of making your own flashcards (either a printer and laminator or thick black felt-tip pen and white card).

Now that your child has a working awareness of the letters and their sounds, it's time to move on to the second stage of learning to read: learning to recognise and read **whole words**. This is an immensely rewarding and exciting time; the thrill of seeing your child recognise his first printed word can only be matched by his delight in the discovery.

During this stage, we have three main aims:

- to make your child print aware;
- to teach him to recognise familiar words; and
- to allow him to discover the basic building blocks of written language.

This may sound like heavy going ... be assured that it is not! The hard work has already been done by us; for you and your baby it's just a question of more games, more fun, more interaction.

But first, let's take a look at some of the thinking behind what we're going to do.

Becoming print aware

As adults, you'll have been reading for so many years that looking at the print on a page will have become not just second nature but utterly automatic.

Now try this thought experiment. Imagine you have had your memory wiped entirely clean and you have to start again with nothing but your native intelligence. Someone comes to entertain you with a book. You see a picture of a cat with a furry white tummy and a mat in a beautiful red colour. In the background you see a few more details of the room and in the corner there's a fish in a bowl. At the bottom in the corner there are a few black lines and dots. The person who has come to read to you says:

"The cat sat on the mat!"

"Ah yes!" you think. "I know why they're saying that. They're not just picking any old words out of the air. They're saying 'cat' because there's a picture of a cat. And they're saying 'mat' because there's a picture of a mat. And 'sat' tells me what the cat's doing – yes! I can see that the cat *is* sitting on the mat. *Now* I understand how this thing called a book works. We look at the pictures and we talk about what we see".

This is an intelligent and thoughtful response. It is quite clear that there is a link between the pictures you see and the words you hear and you have come to a sensible conclusion. Indeed, it would be just plain weird if you were to ignore the link between the picture and the words and conclude that it was the black lines and dots that had prompted your reader to tell you about the cat and the mat.

Your child is in exactly this situation. It's not lack of intelligence, nor even lack of ability that prevents him from picking up reading at an early age without any help from you. It's just that he is not print aware – virtually all baby-focussed material directs his attention *away* from the link between print and meaning, and the link is not an intuitive one.

So, what to do? Should you throw out all your beautiful baby books with lovingly produced illustrations, varied textures and intriguing lift-the-flaps? Emphatically **not**! They are marvellous for your baby's development. But be aware that they are helping your baby with the literacy strand of the Baby Phonics Method. They are not, in themselves, helping your baby to master the technical aspect of reading.

Flashcards

For this technical aspect, you will need to make flashcards on roughly a monthly basis. When making your flashcards, make sure that you make them:

- very plain and simple; just a black word on a white background

- without illustrations or any other distinguishing features
- using a clear font, preferably one which uses the rounded "a", rather than the more complex "a"

Flashcards made in this way are designed to help your baby become print aware; to realise that print *speaks*. When you show your baby a flashcard that says simply:

cat

his mind will be busy trying to make a link between what you're saying and what he's seeing. There are no red herrings for him to catch on to – he can't think that you're saying it in response to a picture of a cat because there *is* no picture. He can't be looking at the fancy design of the card because there *is* no fancy design. He'll *have* to conclude that it is these black squiggles which are making you say "cat", because (quite simply) you've left him no other conclusion to come to. Bravo! This is print awareness – a major conceptual step along the path of learning to read.

Recognising familiar words

Alongside becoming print aware, repeated exposure to these flashcards will allow your baby to start looking at the pattern and shape of the whole word and to make the link between that particular shape and the particular word he hears. This is an important skill to develop, especially in English where (unfortunately) a significant proportion of words cannot be decoded by using the phonic rules.

Discovering the building blocks

However, as you might expect, we believe that it is vital that children have an awareness of the **phonics rules** – the building blocks of the written language. Is your baby too young to be taught any kind of formal rules? Yes, of course … and it would be pretty dull as well. Is your baby too young to work them out for himself, given the appropriate materials? Not in the slightest.

If this seems like a large claim, just consider what your baby's brain is managing to process in terms of language. Even a language with a relatively simple grammar such as English has a lot of grammatical rules to learn. In another year or so you'll hear your child say, "Look! There are some sheeps", or "I seed a ship", or "Jack throwed a ball". These little mistakes tell us volumes about the type of learning that has gone on. Your child is not just imitating what he hears (how often do you talk about "sheeps"?) but he is working out rules and applying them to new situations. He has **learned** that plurals are made by adding an -s to the end of a singular word, and that we put things in the past tense by adding -ed, and he can **apply** these rules. Children in other countries have even harder rules to learn. Polish children, for example, have to learn that words following the numbers 1 to 4 take the accusative case, but words following the numbers 5 and over go in the genitive ... until they get to 11, 12, 13 and 14 when it's back to the accusative. The thought of learning such rules strikes terror into the heart of the average adult, but learn them the children do and apply them they do ... without any kind of formal grammatical teaching.

So the ability to learn and apply relatively complicated rules is just a normal and natural part of growing up. The Baby Phonics Method works with this natural process and allows your child to intuit and internalise the phonics rules by providing him with a number of examples of each rule in his day-to-day life.

Enough of the theory: what about the practice?

How do I start?

First, you need to choose the best first words for your baby. At the start, the focus is on engaging your baby's attention through the flashcards, so we suggest beginning with words which are important to your child. Typically, these will be your child's own name, "mummy", "daddy", the names of siblings or other carers, the names of favourite toys or characters, or words such as "kiss" and "hug" ... but you can choose the most appropriate ones for your child. Then make up two sets of flashcards of the first four words.

Once you have your flashcards, take one set and stick them up on the wall at adult height. Ideally, this should be an area you pass frequently during the day and is clear of other things which might distract your baby, such as light switches, children's paintings and the like. Then hoist your baby up and let him see the flashcard. If it takes his attention at that moment, he'll reach out for it, and whatever he reaches for, name it. So, "Jake" (as he points), "that says 'Jake'" (as he grabs), "Jake, Jake, Jake, Jake, Jake" (as he fights with you to rip it off the wall).

Attention grabbing

If your baby reaches out for the card before naming it, you'll be sure that it has his full attention and you can go full steam ahead. However, if *you* point to the card, it's vital to make sure that he's actually looking at it before saying anything about it. Often, just a couple of taps are needed to redirect your baby's attention. Remember, there's **absolutely no point** naming the card while he's spotting a crumb on the floor or watching the cat rip up today's newspaper. What connections can your baby make from that?

Pretty quickly, your baby will lose interest in the look-and-name process. Absolutely fine. Move on – go and push some cars around or chase a ball. But the next time you pass the wall, do it again. It's not the length of time that you spend doing this, but the **frequency** and **regularity** that matter. Frequent exposure will build the words into your baby's environment in a way that intensive teaching never can.

And that says ... ?

After your baby has had a good look at the words on the wall for a while – say a week or so – ask "Where does it say 'mummy'?". If he points to the right word then heap on the praise in a big way. Don't be fooled – to a large degree it'll be the position of the word on the wall that he's remembering – but a correct answer gives you the opportunity to lavish on the praise and make much of him. He'll be pleased that you're pleased, especially if you make it very obvious. "*Who's* a clever reader? *Dan's* a clever reader". Etc, etc. Setting him up to win and then making much of him when he does lays good foundations for enjoying playing with the flashcards.

Once he seems to be able to find the word on a regular basis, try changing the position of the cards on the wall. If he can still find the right word even after you've moved it, you can be pretty sure that he's learnt to recognise the word itself. If not, just carry on talking about it as before.

There's one big caveat here, however. If your child doesn't know the answer he may well try to guess, pointing out a word at random. If you can, try to prevent this happening. As we've said in earlier chapters, a wrong guess forms a wrong link in your child's mind and this is clearly counter-productive. It's quite tempting sometimes to keep hanging on, hoping that your child will get the right answer if you wait around... but do try to resist the temptation. If he doesn't know the answer, just show him. He'll know it soon enough.

And the others?

We mentioned earlier that you'll need to make two copies of each flashcard. The extra set are not to go on the wall but to be kept loose with your toys. As you already do with the letters, incorporate these words into the games you play together. Anything you can do which draws your baby's attention to the word whilst he looks at it is good (as before, you'll find some suggestions for games in the *Suggested Activities* section). Sometimes these games will be little more than putting the cards on the floor and naming them; other times you may be having a tug-o-war with the 'mummy', or be down on all fours, racing towards the 'hippopotamus'.

At quieter times, you may find that your child is receptive to simply sitting on your lap and listening to you read through the flashcards in order. "Mummy / Daddy / Peter / Flopsy Bunny / Mummy / Daddy / Peter / Flopsy Bunny ...". It's a bit of a thrill for children in a complicated, adult world to find that they fully understand something for the first time. Flashcards are simple to understand and often children enjoy looking at them for their own sake, without the trappings of a game. There is nothing a baby this age likes more than linking names with objects. It is, after all, the way he's learning to talk.

Becoming more advanced

As you make up each month's flashcards, consider whether your child has any fresh enthusiasms. If he does (say, he's developed a passion for playing shops) then make up flashcards with the names of things he might buy, plus perhaps "trolley", "till". You'll then find it much easier to incorporate the cards into his games. And favourite foods and drinks are always winners.

More and more, however, we suggest you lead your baby through some of the basic phonics rules with the flashcards. The progression should be along these lines:

- 3 months of words which can be sounded out simply by knowing the letter sounds – eg "c-a-t"
- 3 months of words which use digraphs – eg "sh", "th", "wh"
- 3 months of words which use a final 'e' to lengthen the middle vowel – eg "plane", "cake"
- 3 months of words with a variety of different rules – eg 'y' used as a vowel, the sound of certain diphthongs.

Along the way, add in some of the basic "sight" words – words which everyone needs to know and no-one can deduce – eg "you", "we", "go", "water".

Please remember that you never have to teach your baby these rules. Nor do you need to be particularly familiar with the theory yourself. All you need to do is to be able to read the words and help your baby become familiar with them, using the games and methods that work best for you. If your baby is engaging with the words and hearing you say the appropriate sounds then he will start to deduce the rules for himself ... by far the best way to learn.

Recognising different fonts

There is one final hurdle for your baby to overcome in respect to word-recognition. As an adult, you almost certainly process the various fonts you see around you without a second thought. For a child, however, different fonts can pose a very real additional challenge. For instance, up until now, we have been teaching your child that an 'a' looks like this:

So what is he to think when he comes across a letter written like this?:

There is no intuitive reason at all why these two letters should be the same and the first time your child comes across the different form he won't have a clue what the letter says. A "g" can also be written in two different ways. These little things which seem insignificant to an adult eye can really throw your child when he first comes across them.

So, once your child is well underway with the flashcards, we suggest you make up the cards in two different fonts each month. You can use these flashcards in exactly the same way as you used the previous ones, but seeing the same word written two different ways will help your child realise that while fonts change, spellings do not.

And once again ...
Dos and Don'ts

- **Don't** stop playing with the letters and looking at the abc book and flashcards. Children forget as easily as they learn and it would be such a shame for all of your early work to slip away through lack of use.

- **Do** try to look at the flashcards several times each day – ideally each time you pass the wall.

- **Do** heap on the praise and make the flashcards fun and rewarding.

- **Do** help him to develop his concentration skills by restricting TV viewing and time spent with over-stimulating battery-powered toys.

Moving on
By the end of this stage, your child should have built up a bank of words that he can recognise at sight. All that is left is to learn how to transfer these skills to word recognition in books ... we'll discuss this on the next stage of the Baby Phonics Method course.

MAKING PROGRESS
CHAPTER 9: DEVELOPING LITERACY SKILLS

What you will need for this section:

- A selection of story books
- A songs and rhymes CD

You have already invested a great deal of time and enjoyment introducing your baby to books. He can now select books that he wants to share with you and he understands that when you are reading, he is looking and listening. He knows that some books have exciting flaps to open, and others will make you put on a silly voice that will make him laugh. He enjoys listening to rhymes and songs and he wants to babble along as you sing. This is all great! Please don't stop any of this now that he is one. Having fun with books, language and rhyme is the single best thing you can do to lay the foundations for a lifelong love of literacy.

Below we have outlined a few more suggestions to extend what you are already doing and to maximise your child's enjoyment of books. Once again we have divided this up into ideas for **shared time** (when you are reading or playing together) and **independent time** (when he is entertaining himself discovering the world you have given him).

Approximately 12-18 months
Shared time: Books

As your child reaches the big milestone – his first birthday - there are likely to be some changes to his routine that you can use to help develop his literacy awareness. Many mothers stop breast feeding at 12 months and children who are bottle fed change to a 'sucky cup' or a cup with a straw. Suddenly your child is able to read a book **whilst** drinking his milk. Why not make the most of this? Keep a basket of books by your bed to share in the morning and use the comfy chair in the nursery for evening 'milk and story'. In this way, you are beginning a lovely routine that can continue throughout his childhood. Before you know it you will be reading three or four stories at bedtime and your child will realise that demands for a "**STORWY**!" are a great way to put off actually having to go to sleep!

Your child will get the most out of anything by getting to know it back-to-front (and front-to-back and upside-down as well). This being so, it is really important that your child gets to know a handful of quality texts inside out. Yes, it is (of course) worthwhile to share a wide range of stories and rhymes, but this is the icing on the cake. The cake itself consists of having a few core books that you share over and over again which can sink deep into your child's consciousness. A simple story that scans well, has lovely rhythm and which rhymes will be wonderful for your child to hear repeatedly. After all, it is only by hearing and learning such language that they will be able to reproduce it themselves. Once again you may be amazed how many times your child will want to hear a story. In fact you might find that the moment you have finished reading a particular book they will demand that it is read 'again' ... and again ... and again.

Shared time: Songs and rhymes
But, as you know, reading books together is only part of developing your child's literacy. Singing songs and rhyming rhymes with your child helps him to develop an ear for the music and patterns in language and so it is really important that you continue to bring these into his life as much as you can. As your child becomes more familiar with the songs, he may start to join in with the actions and words. At twelve months you will probably be guiding his actions with your hands, but it is incredible how quickly he will start to copy and remember. From the start, he will certainly love to babble along and delight in clapping his hands to celebrate his achievements at the end.

Many parents find it helpful to fit the rhymes and songs into their daily routine. 'Rub-a-dub-dub' is a great one for bath time. 'Here we go round the Mulberry bush' is ideal as you get up in the morning, with an infinite number of appropriate verses ('this is the way we wash our face / brush our teeth / pull Daddy's toes' etc, etc), and there are many others for key times in between. After a while you will automatically sing at these times and your child will **want** to join in with the words and actions.

Shared time: Journeys

Time in the car often seems to be wasted time, but it needn't be. There are many lovely CDs on the market that can be used in the car (and in the home) to encourage familiarity with songs and rhymes. As with books, it's best to choose just one or two that you really like and play them over and over again. You might find yourself getting fed up with 'Mary had a little lamb', or 'The Cat in the Hat', but we guarantee that your child won't be. He will just be absorbing the language, the rhythm and the rhyme.

Independent time: Books

It's important that you continue to provide an environment for your child that will encourage him to choose to look at and enjoy books. Remember to keep your child's books at his level – if they are tucked away out of sight, he will inevitably choose something more readily available to entertain him. By now he will be able independently to enjoy lift-the-flap books, so make sure that you have a wide selection available. They might well get torn and damaged, but half the fun is working together to stick the flaps back in place! Provide him with books that have bold illustrations and just a little text so that he can feel that he is actually reading when he attempts to say what is on each page. Leave his favourite story book on the coffee table, so that he can toddle over to it and choose to read it to himself.

He has now seen you read an enormous number of books to him and he will want to model everything that you do. Your job is simply to facilitate this happening.

Approximately 18 –24 months

Nowadays toddlers seem to have a very busy social life. They have music one morning, gym the next, not to mention art and crafts, swimming and simply visiting friends. So how can we keep books and story telling at the forefront of their lives when they have so much else to distract them?

Shared time: Make-believe

As your child approaches two there is so much scope for fun and games with stories. He is now familiar with a host of traditional tales and there are so many ways of bringing these to life. It just requires a little imagination. For example… when visiting a local park or wood, why not retell the story of the three little pigs? All you need to do is find a few sticks, grass and stones and you can together pretend to build three houses. As you narrate the story, take it in turns to be the big bad wolf and the little pigs. Your child will love to huff and puff in the appropriate places and will thoroughly enjoy running away from you, the big bad wolf, as you chase him through the park. In this way, the story that they have only listened to in the past will become far more real and exciting.

Shared time: Magic Stories

Another lovely way to bring stories to life is by telling what we call **Magic Stories**. A magic story has an obvious beginning: "Once upon a time there was a little boy called Jack…" It might continue with a description of the child: "… who had curly blonde hair and sparkling blue eyes…" and give information about what sort of day it is, be it sunny, stormy etc, to reflect the mood of the potential story. The key to this story is that **your child is the protagonist.** It is he that you have been describing and it is he that is the hero in every story that you tell.

When you first begin telling your child magic stories, keep them simple. Let them simply reflect real life situations and scenarios that he would recognise –for example a trip to visit his grandparents or the seaside. As he gets a little older you can make them more exciting. What is so wonderful is that these stories are always unique to **him**. They are about people he knows and places he might have visited or dreamed about. Why don't he and his friend build an enormous sandcastle that touches the candy floss clouds, or perhaps dig a tunnel to somewhere magical beneath the sea? He is engaged by the familiarity of the characters and excited by the fantastical settings and plot. Magic stories **always** end happily and **he** always saves the day! What's more, the best thing about magic stories is that you can tell them anywhere. In the bath, on the potty, at bedtime, in the car…

Shared time: Rhyme games

As we mentioned earlier, there are some wonderful, simple, repetitive books on the market for children this age. As your child becomes more familiar with them, why not play games with the rhyme? As you are reading, pause at significant points and see if your child can fill in the missing word. You are **not** trying to test him; rather you are giving him the opportunity to play the rhyme game with you. If he doesn't provide you with the word immediately, don't wait for him to guess. Carry on reading. You will soon find that he will know the text off by heart and happily join in when you pause. This is a great way to encourage your child to listen out for rhyme, an important skill when learning to read.

Independent time: Storytelling toys

You have already created a wonderful environment for your child to explore books. They are all around him, accessible to him and regularly shared with him. Now you need to give him the opportunity to **retell stories** through play. He is obviously far too young to tell a story with a beginning, a middle and an end. But he is initiating the story process. He is starting to recreate imaginary situations and is slowly developing the vocabulary to express these ideas for himself.

The best way to develop this is to provide him with toys that will encourage him to make-believe. Give him a few small dolls and a dolls house or a track with some trains and you'll be amazed what happens. The dolls will have exciting adventures and potentially wonderful conversations; the trains will crash and biff and bash, and the start of a story is being made. In this way your child is starting the story process and as he grows, these stories will become more and more elaborate.

In essence, at this age stories and books must be fun. They must be exciting and engaging as there are so many other distractions out there. Your toddler will love to listen to and be a part of stories that are shared in this way.

Dos and Don'ts

- **Do** continue to read stories even though you have so much else to fill your days.

- **Don't** get fed up with reading the same story over and over and **over** again. If your child wants to listen, then indulge him. It is really beneficial.

- **Do** make the most of time spent in the car to listen to taped stories, songs and rhymes.

- **Do** have fun with your child by bringing the stories you all know so well to life. Your child is now ready for 'make believe'.

- **Do** provide your child with toys that encourage imaginative play and **do** play with him at first, so that you can model how to play imaginatively.

CHAPTER 10: SUGGESTED ACTIVITIES

Technical strand

Direct your child's attention to the flashcards on the wall; then tell him what each one says as he reaches for it.

Little and often is the key: try to do this every time you pass the cards with your child.

Play "hide the flashcard" with the loose cards.

"Where can 'cat' be now? Is 'cat' hiding here? How about here? Oh, just *look* where 'cat' was hiding! Look, Tom, 'cat' is just here"

Play 'peepbo' with the flashcards.

If a favourite story uses one of the words your child is learning, try bringing out the card when the word crops up in the story.

"... and then, out of the shadows, crept the ... PIG!!" (as you produce the card).

Try putting a card between the two of you as you have a cuddle and calling it a "[word] sandwich". Ask your child to choose which word to use for a sandwich next.

If your child is interested in drawing, sit him on your lap and ask:
"What shall I write? Shall I write 'mummy' or 'daddy' or 'Freddie'"?
Print very clearly and say each letter as you write it.

If your child is very active, make up some action flashcards. Then play an action game with, say, 'clap', 'crawl' and 'sit'.

At first, you'll need to say the words as you hold up the cards; after a while you can just pause for a second before reading them out; later you can just hold up the cards and watch him respond.

Put one flashcard at the end of the room, then get down on all fours with him and have a crawling race to the 'ship'

At calmer times, sit him on your lap and just read through the flashcards to him without playing any games. Show him the card, say the word; show him the next, say the word ... and keep going for as long as it holds his attention.

Keep the flashcards in a box and unpack them and repack them with him, reading each one as you take it out and put it back in.

When you are out together, point out single words you see, especially if they are clearly displayed and often repeated.

Many water hydrants, for example, are marked on the pavement by a little grating with the word "water". Point it out to your child each time you see one and ask him to jump on it three times (don't forget to count the jumps out loud!). Soon he'll be keen to spot them too.

Many street names are positioned at just the right height for a child. Encourage your child to point to each letter in the sign and tell him what it says. This will start to incorporate capital letters into his knowledge.

Many supermarkets are fantastic for displaying signs in clear print. Spotting words and numbers can make the weekly shop a little less trying for both of you.

Literacy strand

Keep a basket of favourite books by the bed to facilitate early morning story time.

E.g. **Where's my Teddy** by Jez Alborough or **The Gruffalo** by Julia Donaldson.

Snuggle up in bed together and make this a special time each day.

Choose a book such as **We're going on a Bear Hunt** by Michael Rosen and Helen Oxenbury. Read it with your child repeatedly, trying the following:

- Think of an action for each of the descriptive phrases – e.g rub your hands together for 'swishy swashy, swishy swashy'.
- Change the speed as you read, starting slowly as you build up to meeting

the bear and then read really quickly as you run away from it.

- Pause at certain points to encourage your child to join in. "We're going on a bear hunt, We're going to catch a _____"
- Go on a bear hunt around the garden. You'll know the story off by heart too, so lead your child through imagined rivers and swamps to a dark corner in your garden and run away from the bear together.

Share modern rhymes with your child – such as **Rumble in the Jungle** by Giles Andrae. These rhymes can be read over and over again as they are humorous and engaging. Try adding a simple tune to add interest or vary your voice to reflect the character of the animal being described.

Sing a simple song, such as **Wind the Bobbin up**. At 12 months, guide his hands so that he can perform the actions. As he gets older, do the actions yourself and see if he can copy you.

Leave out the rhyming word and see if he can fill it in. "Put your hands upon your _____"

Make the most of your environment to encourage story telling and imaginative play. A playhouse in the garden can make a wonderful castle or dungeon or whatever you want to make-believe it into. A slide can be used to represent a beanstalk, as can a washing line or even a tall tree! Be creative, be imaginative and your child will have a lot of fun.

If your child has picked up language particularly quickly and is enjoying talking, try providing him with some puppets so that he can begin to retell traditional stories himself.

Tell your child magic stories whenever you can.

Remember, they always start in the same way and they will always be about your child.

"Once upon a time there was a little boy called Charlie. He had dark hair and green eyes and loved to play in his garden. One stormy afternoon, Charlie…"

You know what your child likes, so make your stories relevant and interesting to him. Tell them anywhere and everywhere.

CHAPTER 11: PRODUCT RECOMMENDATIONS

By the time your child's first birthday has crept around, you may well feel that you have acquired as much child-related clutter as you can possibly handle. Nonetheless, unless you are possessed of an iron will, you will inevitably acquire much, much more during your child's second year. The following are some suggestions which may help you turn your child-related clutter into Baby Phonics Method related clutter – no tidier, but hopefully more productive.

TECHNICAL STRAND

During this stage, most of the materials you will need for the technical strand of the Baby Phonics Method will be the flashcards you will make. If you buy no other products this year for this strand, it will do no harm at all.

First word books

However, the work you are doing with the flashcards will be reinforced by the use of first word books, and if you have not acquired any over the previous year it may be worth keeping your eye out for some now.

As before, it is best if the words in a first word book are set out:

- in a large, clear font;
- in a straight line;
- in lower-case letters; and
- separate from other words and detail on the page.

Clear print story books

You can also use this time to put in some worthwhile groundwork for the next stage of the Baby Phonics Method by introducing your child to some compelling stories written with clear, bold text. Look for books which:

- have the text written in black on a white (or light) background so that it is easy to read;

- have text written in clear straight lines;
- don't have too much text on a page;
- (if possible) repeat easy words several times; and
- are enjoyable.

Often reading scheme books are very well-written and fulfil these criteria admirably; equally it is not too difficult to find mainstream story books which comply.

We recommend:

- **Mr Pod and Mr Picalilli** Penny Dolan and Nick Sharratt
- **Eight Enormous Elephants** Penny Dolan and Leo Bradley
- All the books in the **Red Nose Readers** series
- Books in the **Leapfrog Fairy Tales** series
- Stories from the **Read It Yourself** series published by Ladybird
- Many of the **In the Night Garden** books

LITERACY STRAND

As before, there are hundreds of fantastic books that you could buy to reinforce the literacy strand. But don't forget, it is important for your child to read a few quality texts over and over again. Below we have outlined a range of texts and CDs for you to choose from. All are fantastic, so simply choose the ones that you and your child like best.

Lift-the-flap and board books

Now that your child has reached his first birthday, these books are ideal for independent exploration. As well as the books we recommended for the previous stage we suggest you look at:

- **I'm Hungry** Rod Campbell
- **Peekaboo Park!** Emily Bolam
- **Each Peach Pear Plum** Janet and Alan Ahlberg

Repetitive texts

Don't forget these classics, now that your child is that little bit older. He will enjoy the repetition, and may begin to join in with you as you read. We recommend:

- **The Very Lonely Firefly** Eric Carle
- **The Very Hungry Caterpillar** Eric Carle
- **We're Going On a Bear Hunt** Michael Rosen and Helen Oxenbury

Books to encourage songs and rhymes

These books are great now that your child is beginning to learn language and can join in too.

- **The Wheels on the Bus** Kate Merritt
- **Wind the Bobbin Up (Hands on Songs)** Anthony Lewis
- **Lucy Cousin's Big Book of Nursery Rhymes** Lucy Cousins
- **Ten Green Bottles** Tamsin Hinrichsen
- **Old Macdonald had a Farm** Francesca Stick and Jemima Lumley

Longer texts for quiet moments

We have previously suggested that you might like to introduce a morning and evening story time with your child. Put together a selection of lovely stories that you and he will enjoy sharing over and over again.

- **The Tiger who Came to Tea.** Judith Kerr
- **My Friend Bear** or **Where's my Teddy?** Jez Alborough
- **Big Blue Train** Julia Jarman and Adrian Reynolds
- **Monkey Puzzle** Julia Donaldson
- **Hairy Maclary's Caterwaul Caper** and other stories by Lynley Dodd

Audio books and CDs of rhymes and songs

These are wonderful to play in the car, to share quietly with your child or to introduce at bedtime.

- **The Cat in the Hat and other stories** Dr. Seuss and Adrian Edmondson
- **Rumble in the Jungle (Book and CD)** Giles Andreae and David Wojtowycz
- **The Smartest Giant in Town (Book and CD)** Julia Donaldson
- **Wheels on the Bus (Pre-school songs) BBC Audio**
- **Incy Wincy Spider (Book and CD) BBC Audio**

If you would like to discuss the merits of these, or any other product you have found then please email a Baby Phonics Method consultant or mention it at your next phone call.

This is the end of the *Making Progress* section.

Once you have read these chapters, we highly recommend you contact one of our consultants for a half hour phone conversation.

Can't manage a phone call during working hours? Just let us know when you book; we have some weekend and evening slots available.

Phone calls call be booked through our website www.babyphonicsmethod.com and cost £30 for a half hour call.

We hope to speak to you soon!

the
baby phonics
method

BECOMING AN INDEPENDENT READER

from approximately 24 months onwards

BECOMING AN INDEPENDENT READER
CHAPTER 12: INDEPENDENT TECHNICAL SKILLS

What you will need for this section:

- A copy of **Mr Pod and Mr Piccalilli** by Penny Dolan and Nick Sharratt (or other appropriate book)

Is your child reading a fair number of words from flashcards? Is he spotting an occasional word he recognises in petrol stations, supermarkets or from trains? Do you enjoy sharing stories together? If so, it is time to move your child onto this, the third and final stage of the Baby Phonics Method.

The aim of this stage is to bring together all the skills your child has learnt so far and apply them to the challenge of reading books; initially with a lot of help from you, and finally by himself. Once your child can decode a book (even a very basic) book alone, he has a grip on the skills he'll use through his life to read reading-scheme books, textbooks, history books, dissertations, Prime Ministerial briefings ...

Choosing the right book

As ever, choosing the right materials can make your child's task significantly easier. We suggest you invest in a copy of **Mr Pod and Mr Piccalilli** by Penny Dolan and Nick Sharratt. This is our favourite text for this stage for four main reasons:

- The text is clear and is in straight lines on a plain background
- It uses repetition liberally ... but not at the expense of the story
- Many of the key words in the story are easy words to learn
- It it beautifully illustrated and appealingly presented.

However, it is up to you to see if the fifth and most important element is present:

- Your child enjoys the story.

If not, then despite all its advantages, this will not be the book for him. It is crucial to find a story which your child enjoys and wants to hear again and again. If this book isn't for you, take a look at the **Product Recommendations** section for some alternatives, or choose your own, bearing the above criteria in mind. This chapter is written with the assumption that you are using the **Mr Pod** book, but everything we say can be applied equally to any other clearly written text targeted at roughly the same level.

What do I do?

The first step is to familiarise your child with the book. So over the first week or so, read it through together as many times as you can. Make sure you always read the text (rather than improvising), and let your child have a good look at the pictures and enjoy the story. The first goal is to encourage your child to enjoy the book and to get an ear for the rhythm and shape of the story.

Blankety Blank

Once the story has become a favourite, you can start to leave out a word and see if your child can fill it in for you. For example, you might start reading, "Mr Pod lived on a first floor flat. He lived all alone and kept himself to himself, but he did have a …?". If you make it clear by your tone and expression that you're encouraging your child to join in, he will hopefully finish the sentence with "...CAT!!"

As he does so you need to **draw his attention** to the word "cat" on the page. You can point to it yourself, use his finger to point to it, or do anything else that works in the circumstances. The important thing is that when he says "Cat!" he is also looking at the word "cat" on the page.

Then carry on reading the story. From your child's point of view you are reading him a story, not teaching him, and this is the way it should be.

The story continues with Mr Piccalilli, and you can do the same again. "Mr Piccalilli lived on a ground floor flat. He lived all alone and kept himself to himself, but he did have a …?"

Later on, there are more opportunities to point out "cat": "Oh dear! Have you seen my …?". So, whenever the word "cat" appears at a key point in the sentence, you can ask your child to fill in for you. So long as he is **looking** at the word at the same time as **saying** it, he is not just reciting but beginning to read it.

After you have read the book like this a fair number of times, you can turn to a page and ask "Where's 'cat'?" If you're lucky, he'll look for the word rather than the picture. If you're extremely lucky, he'll point it out to you. This is real word-recognition and it's a big achievement. It's worth reinforcing it by looking for other instances of the word scattered around the book.

If he doesn't look for it or find it, just gently point it out to him and try again another day. There's no rush.

As ever, it's best to start slowly and at first concentrate on just one or two different words at a time. But once your child has got the idea and is enjoying the game, you can ask him to fill in a number of different words. In the **Mr Pod** book, easy words which work well with this technique include *flat, Tod, Millie, high, low, not, sad, cake, miaow, kittens, joy, happy*, and these are lovely words to add to your child's reading vocabulary.

Once you've got the key words taped you can see if your child can fill in some of the surrounding words; perhaps "first-floor flat" instead of just "flat", or "loved Tod" instead of just "Tod".

Eventually, if the book sustains your child's interest, he may be able to match up all the words of the story to the printed text. Every time he does this he's teaching himself to read, using a book that he enjoys, and reinforcing the idea that printed words have a meaning attached. It's great progress!

Other books
Not many children (or their parents!) will want to limit themselves to just one book for months on end; neither would we recommend doing so. The more books you can share together the better. But with every book which your child enjoys and which has fairly clear text, we suggest going through the three stages of:

- familiarisation
- filling in words
- spotting the words on a page.

Clearly, the more books to which your child is exposed, the more words he is likely to pick up … so, read, read, read!

What about the flashcards?

You will have accumulated quite a bundle of flashcards by now, and it would be a shame to let your child forget them. So we recommend keeping them around and continuing to play with them for another year or so. If you come across a word in a book which matches one of the flashcards, then your child might like to get the card out and see one of "his" words in a "real" book.

However, the more your child starts picking up on words in books, the less necessary the flashcards become. Their primary purpose was to help your child become print aware, but you now have a big tick in that box. So, feel free to gradually phase them out as you expose your child more and more to words from other sources.

Reading alone

You may have thought that your child had outgrown the baby board books, targeted at the very early ages … hopefully, you haven't yet given them to the charity shop. Once children begin to be able to read words, they love being able to read whole books alone. At the beginning, age-appropriate stories will be beyond them, but some baby books use a very limited vocabulary. A book which reads *"Where's baby? Here he is!"* repeated throughout will become accessible very soon; take advantage of it!

Reading scheme books

We are often asked, "Should I be starting Johnny on a reading scheme?" Our answer is … it depends. Reading scheme books have many advantages: they're clear, structured and they use simple words – we've recommended some in the **Product Recommendations** section. However, at this stage, the key to success is enjoyment. If the book isn't holding your child's attention, then you'll do far better with a book that he loves and from which he can pick up a few words. There's no pressure when a child is learning at this age, and so if he learns words in an unstructured or haphazard way, it really doesn't matter. A little girl who loves ponies is perfectly entitled to learn "gymkhana" before she learns "car". If that's what she enjoys, why not?

It is also worth bearing in mind that most schools use the Oxford Reading Tree and are not always happy if children come to school having already read their reading books. Recognising this, the scheme has produced "Read at Home" spin-offs, and if your child's prospective school uses the scheme it will probably be better to stick to these.

You can find a modern spin on the traditional reading scheme approach by checking out www.starfall.com This exceptional free phonics website has a remarkable variety of games, stories and puzzles, all based on phonics. It has material aimed at all levels, from learning the letter sounds, right through to year 2 level literacy. We have yet to find a child who can't find something to their taste on here and it is as structured as any reading scheme.

Television

Up until now, we've been recommending that you keep TV viewing to a minimum, and we're not changing that advice now. It is (in our opinion) **always more productive** to share a book or play a game than it is to watch TV.

Nonetheless, we recognise that most children will be watching some TV by this age, and there are a few simple things you can do to make the experience more educational (without making it any less enjoyable or relaxing):

- Try to record programmes and let your child get to know some favourites in detail, rather than always watching live TV.
- If you can, try to guide your child towards the slower paced programmes (eg Charlie & Lola, Barnaby Bear, Something Special, Step Inside, In The Night Garden, Numberjacks) rather than the super-stimulating fast moving ones (eg LazyTown, Mister Maker, most cartoons).
- Try to favour CBeebies. No rule is absolute, but generally the programmes on CBeebies are better than those elsewhere.

The last tip is so helpful it deserves a section to itself:

- If you have the capability, put the subtitles on every time the TV is on.

Widely available subtitles are a marvellous development in children's television. Your child will be reading what he hears all the time he is watching … a little bit of education slipped in through the back door, and at no cost to anyone.

And at last, the final set of technical …

Dos and Don'ts

- **Do** take every opportunity to read books together.

- **Do** look out for books with clear, accessible text.

- **Do** stick to books your child enjoys.

- **Do** put the subtitles on the TV.

- **Do** play on <u>www.starfall.com</u>

- **Don't** put the flashcards away straight away.

BECOMING AN INDEPENDENT READER
CHAPTER 13: INDEPENDENT LITERACY SKILLS

What you will need for this section:

- A selection of longer books
- Some audio books
- Props for independent storytelling

Your child has now been exposed to a wide variety of stories and texts and has absorbed more of the language and content of these stories than you can possibly imagine. His imagination has been **fired** and he is now ready to reproduce, in his own way, all the imaginative content that you have given to him. The magic stories that you have told, the repeated readings of his favourite tales, the hours of audio CDs that you have played and the songs and rhymes that you have sung are now going to start revealing themselves as he plays. At his age, the majority of his play will be imaginative and your child has a wealth of creative experiences and language to influence the imaginary worlds he creates. Much of this play will be narrated and you may be amazed at what you hear.

None the less, there are still plenty of activities that you can do with your child to continue this growth, and in this chapter we will give some examples of how you can continue with and build on what you have already done to develop your child's love of stories.

Shared time: Short stories

As your child gets older, he will be more able to listen to longer texts without the need for pictures to scaffold his understanding of what is happening and to engage his interest. Longer texts really develop a child's listening and comprehension skills and can be easily incorporated into his daily routine. There are certain times of the day when a quiet read is really beneficial, especially as your child is now reaching the age when he will be dropping his daytime nap and will need periods of 'down time' to keep him going until bedtime. Here are some general guidelines to help make this a success.

- At first choose a book with short stories so that your child can listen to a whole story in one go and not just a chapter. A nice example would be **Old Bear and his Friends** by Jane Hissey. There are illustrations, but only one or two per story and they don't relate much to the action. Your child has to use his imagination to picture what is happening, as the details are in the descriptions and not the illustrations.
- Recap regularly what has happened. At appropriate moments make a comment or ask a question to ensure that your child has understood. For example: "Little Bear is really upset, isn't he? Why do you think he's so sad?"
- Encourage your child to think that he is really clever to be listening to a story without pictures. Praise him and make him want to listen to more.
- It goes without saying really… make sure there are no other distractions whilst you are reading. A younger sibling playing with a noisy toy or a telly in the background will be too much of a distraction at first.

Shared time: Chapter books

Once your child has experienced a lot of short stories, he will be ready to listen to longer texts with chapters. He will need a certain level of maturity for this to be a success and probably be well over three years old before the following suggested texts and activities are appropriate.

There are some wonderful stories available for children that you will thoroughly enjoy sharing with your child. Any easy Roald Dahl book will certainly fire your child's imagination, as will Dick King Smith and AA Milne. As your child gets more mature you will be able to read a longer text over a period of weeks. Make the reading of the book a really special activity that can be looked forward to with anticipation. Maybe keep it for bedtime, but keep it alive in your child's mind through out the day by asking "I wonder what's going to happen tonight?"

Once a child is absorbed in a longer text you are in the perfect position to develop their literacy skills. Pose questions to encourage your child's prediction skills. "What do you think will happen next?" "If you were x, what would you do now?" At first your child will undoubtedly say "I don't know", but help them learn this skill by modelling it yourself. "I think that …"

"Perhaps … could happen." It is only by listening to you making up possible/impossible scenarios that your child will understand the skill of prediction. What is key to your child being willing to participate, is that he should understand that we don't have to be able to say what is **actually** going to happen, but what could **possibly** happen. The fear that they might get it wrong is enough to stop a child making any sort of guess, so they need to be reassured that any answer is possible. Praise any attempts at predictions, but really go to town praising suggestions that are plausible within the context of the story. If your child can do this, he is well on the way to being a sophisticated reader.

Shared time: Magic stories (Part 2!)

By now you will be very proficient at telling Magic Stories. Your child will have heard so many that he will be familiar with their structure and therefore be ready to start giving you information to include in the story. When you feel that he is ready to be more proactive when it comes to storytelling, include him in the planning stages of the story. "Where will our story take place today?" "What do you think the weather will be like?" Encourage him to think about how his suggestions could affect what happens in the story. "If the wind is blowing and you are on the beach, what might happen to the waves? Where might the rough sea sweep you" etc.

Once he has had plenty of experience creating stories with you in this way, he

may feel confident enough to start telling his own. He probably won't want an audience when he feels brave enough to do this for the first time and he will undoubtedly repeat a story that he has heard you tell, but provide him with a safe and private place to give it a go. Suggest he tells a younger sibling a magic story to cheer them up, or maybe even a favourite teddy bear or doll. Hover nearby to prompt, encourage and praise where necessary but give him the time to be creative himself. Once he has told one, albeit briefly and without perhaps a middle and end, he will be more confident to try again in future. As with all things, the more he tells, the better he will get.

Independent time: Audio books

Another fantastic way of developing your child's ability to concentrate when listening to stories without pictures is to play recordings of extended stories. Once again, the car is a perfect place to encourage this skill. Your child is trapped, in a particularly unexciting environment with no distractions; it is the ideal place for him to absorb himself in a story. There are marvellous productions available of stories such as 'Winnie the Pooh', 'The Wind in the Willows', 'My Naughty Little Sister' and 'Paddington' to name but a few. A long journey can fly past when listening to such stories.

Another time that can feel like a treat is bedtime. After saying goodnight, put a story on for your child to listen to as they are falling asleep. Once again, there are no distractions. It is dark and they are sleepy. As long as you choose wisely (the story must be gentle and familiar) your child will love falling asleep to the words of a beautiful story. What is more, it is minimum effort on your part, but maximum enjoyment for your child!

Independent time: Puppet shows

As we have already said, children need to have the opportunity to practise storytelling **without** an audience. What better way than to provide puppets of familiar characters that your child can use to recreate stories that he knows off by heart. There is no need for adult involvement in this activity. Ensure the puppets are accessible and available and then he can independently select the characters that he needs for his story and quietly enact it by himself. By now, he will most likely be a fantastic narrator and you can enjoy standing back watching him recreate all the stories that you have told him. At times he may even wish to perform his stories to you. Why not invest in a puppet theatre to really encourage these skills? If your child feels that he is putting on a performance, you might even hear a different kind of language, demonstrating an awareness of you as an audience.

Independent time: Old familiar texts

Even though your child is now listening to longer texts, don't forget about the old favourites. Keep them accessible. Some of these books your child will know off by heart and this can turn into a lovely activity which you can encourage. Rather than turning the telly on when your child is tired and in need of a rest, provide him with these familiar stories to look at independently. He may quietly flick through the pages, studying the pictures, but more likely he will tell the story to himself. Either way he is absorbing the content and getting something valuable from these favourite books. More, you are developing in him the realisation that books and stories are a form of relaxation, a quiet activity to be enjoyed independently and this is a valuable lesson to learn.

Do's and Don'ts

- **Do** start to share longer texts with your child.

- **Don't** have too many distractions when you are reading longer texts. Your child needs to be able to picture what is happening and will find this very difficult if there is a telly on in the background or noisy games being played elsewhere.

- **Don't** expect your child to be able to listen immediately to longer chapter books. Prepare him for this by sharing many short stories first.

- **Do** encourage your child to help you tell magic stories.

- **Do** play audio books in the car to encourage listening skills.

- **Do** provide puppets for your child to play with so that he can practise his storytelling.

- **Don't** throw away the old favourites, just because your child is enjoying a longer text.

BECOMING AN INDEPENDENT READER
CHAPTER 14: SUGGESTED ACTIVITIES

Technical strand

Choose a flashcard and try to find that word in a book.

Look for familiar words on street signs ("One Way" or "Give Way" are quite easy to point out)

Look for words in supermarkets which your child might recognise. A trip down the aisle headed "dog food" might be productive even if you don't have a pet.

Use the library to browse for books which might appeal to your child.

Leave very easy books in your child's bed for him to read to himself before he goes to sleep or when he wakes up.

Make a rule that the TV never goes on without the subtitles.

Play on www.starfall.com regularly.

Play I-spy in quiet moments in the car. If it's tricky at the moment, turn it around and ask your child to "guess" with which letter your chosen object begins.

Literacy strand

Over a period of days, share a book of **short** stories with your child. Look at the contents page together and decide which of the stories he might like to listen to. Talk to him about what each story might be about… take suggestions from him and praise his ideas, however unlikely they may be.

Continue to tell your child plenty of Magic Stories. Use the term with your child… "I am going to tell you a Magic Story.." so that he can request one whenever he is in the mood (and you are feeling creative!)

Remember car journeys are ideal opportunities for these stories to be told.

Encourage your child to be involved in the planning stages of a story. Ask pertinent questions, such as "Where shall our story take place today?" or "Who shall be in our story?"

If he helps you plan a story, he will gradually learn to tell stories too.

Listen to audio books together and apart, and enjoy!

Provide a puppet theatre (or a few puppets) for your child to play with. Give him the opportunity to tell stories himself.

Retell traditional stories, such as Little Red Riding Hood or Jack and the Beanstalk with your child as the main character. Little George could fight the giant for a change and your child will love being the hero!

TECHNICAL STRAND

As your child starts to read the words in books it is more vital than ever that you try to find clear books with bold, distinct type. Books with text in swirly patterns or in a colour which doesn't stand out from the background will be of limited help at this stage.

We recommend:

- **Mr Pod and Mr Picalilli** Penny Dolan and Nick Sharratt
- Books in the **In The Night Garden** series which do not have distracting extras (such as buttons for noises or stickers). Eg **Upsy Daisy Loves the Ninky Nonk** Andrew Davenport
- **Some Dogs Do** Jez Alborough
- **One Clever Creature** Joseph Ellis and Christyan Fox
- Anything from the **Red Nose Readers** series
- **Eight Enormous Elephants** Penny Dolan and Leo Bradley
- **One Fish, Two Fish, Red Fish, Blue Fish** or other stories by Dr Seuss

If you would like to try out a reading scheme, we suggest:

- **Red Nose Readers** Allan Ahlberg and Colin McNaughton
- **Leapfrog Fairy Tales**
- **Key Words with Ladybird** (the original Peter and Jane scheme)
- **Oxford Reading Tree Read at Home** Roderick Hunt and Alex Brychta

As your child gets a little older he may enjoy books such as:

- **Mixed Up Fairy Tales** Hilary Robinson and Nick Sharratt
- Anything from the **Animal Babies** series
- **The Cat in the Hat** by Dr Seuss
- **Are You My Mother?** by P.D. Eastman

LITERACY STRAND
Audio Books

When introducing audio books to your child, we suggest you start with a story that is familiar to your child already so that they can visualise the characters. As well, it needs to be relatively short – no more than 10 or 15 minutes long. An ideal example would be:

- **My Completely Best Story Collection** by Lauren Child.

When your child is a little older and has a longer attention span, we recommend:

- **Winnie the Pooh – dramatisation** (Judi Dench, Geoffrey Palmer, Stephen Fry, Jane Horrocks)
- **The Best of Paddington on CD – Complete and Unabridged** by Michael Bond, read by Stephen Fry
- **The Water Horse** by Dick King Smith

Toys to encourage story telling

- **Wooden table top puppet theatre**
- **Puppet Story Sets** by The Puppet Company eg Cinderella

Short Story Collections

Start with **short!** short stories that contain a few illustrations. Good examples would be:

- **The Big Alfie and Annie Rose Story Book** by Shirley Hughes
- **Old Bear and His Friends** by Jane Hissey

Once your child will happily concentrate as your read these, try more challenging texts:

- **The Adventures of Milly Molly Mandy** by Joyce Lankester Brisley

- **Sophie's Snail** by Dick King Smith
- **My Naughty Little Sister** by Dorothy Edwards and Shirley Hughes

Longer texts

The world is really your oyster now. Think back to all the wonderful stories that you enjoyed as a child. We recommend:

- **The Magic Finger** by Roald Dahl
- **The Twits** by Roald Dahl
- **The Sheep-Pig** by Dick King Smith
- **The Owl who was Afraid of the Dark** by Jill Tomlinson

This is the end of the *Becoming an Independent Reader* section.

Once you have read these chapters, we highly recommend you contact one of our consultants for a half hour phone conversation.

Worried about your child's speech development? Ask for a phone consultation with our registered Speech and Language Therapist.

Phone calls call be booked through our website www.babyphonicsmethod.com and cost £30 for a half hour call.

MOVING ON

This is where the Baby Phonics Method course ends. Not, of course, because there is nothing left to do – the process of developing reading skills will continue for years and years to come – but because it will continue along the same lines from here on in. So, our job is done. **Thank you** for joining us and we wish you many happy years of reading together.

GENERAL

CHAPTER 16: QUESTIONS AND ANSWERS

- *What is the Baby Phonics Method?*

The Baby Phonics Method is a method of teaching the basics of reading to children at a very young age. It works on the principle that children best absorb the fundamentals of reading at the age when they absorb the fundamentals of language. The Baby Phonics Method gives your child confidence with print by the time he starts school, allowing him to approach school with enthusiasm.

- *Will the Baby Phonics Method make my child more intelligent?*

Not as such, no. There is no magic bullet which will transform one child into another. Each child is an individual, and will have individual gifts and talents, strengths and weaknesses. However, the Baby Phonics Method is a strong tool to help you to maximise your child's potential. Early reading ability allows children to have confidence in learning and to enjoy it.

- *No-one in my family is academic. Will the Baby Phonics Method still work?*

Yes. The Baby Phonics Method does not require any extraordinary ability on the part of your child. It was devised by an experienced infant school teacher who saw many children struggle with the reading process on arrival at school aged 4 or 5. The Baby Phonics Method simply asks you to provide letters and words as part of your baby's environment. All children learn about the environment into which they are born – it's an essential survival skill. The Baby Phonics Method can ensure that this environment gives them the building blocks for future reading success. Your child may not become the next Prime Minister, brain surgeon or professor, but you can be confident that you are giving him a good chance of getting the most out of his education.

- *I don't think I'm clever enough to teach*

If you have the ability to read this material, then you have enough ability to apply the Baby Phonics Method to your child. The Baby Phonics Method relies on repetition and consistency rather than on complex ideas. As the parent of the child you are already qualified to be his best teacher. You *will* need to spend time interacting with your child. You will *not* need any special ability yourself.

- *I work full-time. How can I apply the Baby Phonics Method to my child?*

Any adult who cares for your child can play the games required by the Baby Phonics Method as part of his daily routine. You will also find your own time (bath time, maybe, or Sunday mornings in bed) when you can contribute to his learning.

- *Will the Baby Phonics Method put too much pressure on my child?*

No. In fact, teaching without pressure is at the heart of the Baby Phonics Method philosophy. Children feel pressured when they feel that their performance is poor compared to that of the children around them or when they are expected to achieve beyond their abilities. The Baby Phonics Method teaches children at an age when they effortlessly absorb concepts and when all their interest is directed to the environment around them. Children only start to compare themselves to their peers much later on. On the Baby Phonics Method, by the time children are old enough to assess themselves against their playmates they should feel proud of, not stressed about, their reading abilities.

- *The Baby Phonics Method requires repetitive teaching. Am I boring my child?*

Learning to read requires repetition. No-one can expect a child – of any age – to link a sound with a letter shape after one telling. Fortunately, babies (unlike older children) love repetition. So, whilst you might find that your five year old will be agitating to get back to his football, you can be sure that repetition of phonic sounds will delight your baby.

- *I've heard that young children can't really learn to read but can only pattern-spot. So how can the Baby Phonics Method work?*

In the early stages at least, learning to read *is* pattern-spotting. Learning letter sounds is pattern-spotting. Recognising basic words is pattern-spotting. This is a fantastic foundation for learning to read. It is true that the ability to apply slightly more complicated rules to analysing a word can only come later. The Baby Phonics Method helps the child to deduce these rules at their own pace.

- *I've been told that in some European countries children don't learn to read until they are 7, and they tend to do much better than English children. Wouldn't it be better to wait?*

Many European countries do indeed start to teach reading at a much later age and have success with their method. Would the same method work here? Not necessarily. These countries are typically ones whose languages have a consistent spelling system. So a child can learn a few rules, and then see them apply in virtually every case. Learning to read these languages is fundamentally an exercise in easy decoding – a perfect task for a seven year old and one which can be mastered in a few days.

Not so in English, however. With our chequered history of invasions and foreign influences our language contains endless numbers of words which just can't be decoded. We eat our "food" and escape from a "flood" ... would you care to explain why the "oo" sound changes? We "love" to "discover" a treasure "trove" … so what's the rule for "-ove"? There certainly are rules to be learnt in English, but there is virtually no rule which doesn't have an exception. Many, many words just have to be learnt, and the most enjoyable way to learn them is through exposure in stories. Unfortunately, exposure takes time, and time is in short supply for a seven year old. A baby, on the other hand, has all the time in the world.

- *Will the Baby Phonics Method help my child at school?*

Definitely. Your child will start school with confidence in his reading abilities and all children love being ahead of their classmates. And although the Baby Phonics Method doesn't claim to make your child more intelligent than he naturally is, a love for learning fostered at an early age can make a great difference to your child's later academic achievements.

- *Will my child be bored if he starts school already able to read?*

Not in the least! Firstly, school is about much more than academic learning. There are numerous social lessons to be learnt and a new environment to explore. This is not a boring time! Secondly, teachers are trained to assess and teach each child as an individual. Each child is given tailored learning goals to develop their existing skills, regardless of how far they have already progressed. So your child's academic schooling should be a process of continual development.

- *If I am teaching letter sounds before my baby can speak, how will I know he is learning them?*

At first, you may not be aware of how much he is learning! But when he can crawl, he may be able to move towards letters when you name them. As his speech develops, you may be surprised that as well as naming the family cat, he can tell you that the letter he is hiding in his nappy is "c".

- *Shouldn't I leave the teaching of reading to my child's school?*

No! Of course, once your child starts school, you will want to co-operate with his teacher and work together to extend his reading skills. However, you can be sure that your child's first teacher will be delighted if he starts school with a knowledge of phonics and an interest in books.

- *Dyslexia runs in my family. How will the Baby Phonics Method affect my child if he is dyslexic?*

We do not claim to be able to cure dyslexia. However, the Baby Phonics Method does have much in common with many leading treatments of dyslexia which focus heavily on early phonic awareness. We have established links with a registered and experienced speech and language therapist who is aware of the advantages of early exposure to phonics. If you have concerns about any aspect of your child's linguistic development, we can arrange for a telephone consultation with our therapist who will discuss your concerns and give you advice on accessing appropriate services.

CHAPTER 17: PUSHY PARENTS

They say that there are only two certainties in this life: death and taxes.

Well, here's a third. If you try to help your baby learn a skill which can even remotely be considered academic, someone, sometime will call you a pushy parent.

The implications of being a pushy parent are horrible. The idea suggests that you are prepared to rob your child of his childhood in order to turn him into a puppet dancing to your tune. It implies that you will prevent his natural development and leave him with severe emotional problems. It suggests that you have little or no sensitivity to your child's needs.

Is this you? Can you even conceive of it being you? The chances are that this description horrifies you (as it does us). Rest assured, then, that **you are not a pushy parent**.

So, why is this term so frequently thrown about? Often, it is motivated by jealousy. It may be used by mums who have brought their children up differently and want to defend their own methods against new ideas. Equally, it may be driven by misconceptions. If people imagine that you are forcing your baby into an Eton collar and sitting him at a desk for hours at a time then they have some genuine concerns. *You* know that you're doing no such thing. Unfortunately, many people have a stubborn tendency to cling to misconceptions and will trumpet the "pushy parent" label regardless of the evidence.

Teaching through play

The "pushy parent" label is rather ironic. The Baby Phonics Method is all about **removing pressure from childhood** and allowing your child to reach his natural potential *without* being pushed. This is because the Baby Phonics Method philosophy is based on two important ideas:

- it is easy to teach a baby vital lifelong skills when he still regards everything he does as play;

- when a child *is* old enough to understand the difference between work and play he will be happiest if work comes easily and play is plentiful.

So, consider which child is more likely to feel "pushed". Is it the 5 year old brought up on the Baby Phonics Method, finding his school-work stress-free and easy, and having plenty of time for vital unstructured play? Or is it the 5 year old brought up on a laissez-faire philosophy who must now buckle down and start the repetitive business of learning phonics .... or not learn to read at all?

Feeding your baby's development

On the Baby Phonics Method you will do no more than build on a baby's natural interests at each stage of his development. You will never try to force him to do something for which he is not ready. If you doubt this, just take a look at what you'll be doing at each stage.

- When your baby is small, he'll love repetition. So, you'll teach him the repetitive sounds of phonics.
- When your baby is a little bigger, he'll love naming things. So, you'll teach him to recognise his first words in print.
- When your baby is a little bigger still, he will be fascinated by making sentences. So, you'll show him how to put together the few words he knows to read his first sentence.
- When your child is a toddler, he'll love creative play and using his imagination. So, you'll show him how to read simple books that spark that imagination.
- When your child is a pre-schooler, his fantasy world will become very real. So, you'll provide him with books which expand and explore his fantasy world.
- When your child starts school, he will finally be required to learn to read. But **he already can**. So, he'll be able to focus on his interests, his play and the social side of school, secure in the knowledge that his reading skills are well-established.

Is this being pushy?

CHAPTER 18: RESEARCH

The Baby Phonics Method is commited to the national ideal that every child should enjoy an early introduction to books. New parents all over the country are being given packs of information about sharing books with their babies and examples of appropriate texts that can be used. Pre-schoolers are often given books when they join their local library. Why has the government funded such a project? It is because there is much evidence to suggest that early access to books and reading will greatly benefit children in the long term.

The key to success in all the activities in the Baby Phonics Method is **enjoyment**, whether it is the playing with the initial alphabetic sounds with the tiny baby or the sharing of a quality text. In his book **Baby Power** Professor Barrie Wade, who has taught in primary and secondary schools as well as being a key proponent of the Book Start project maintains *"Parents have told us how much pleasure they have reading with their children. In short, having fun is a strong motivating factor."*

Critically, there is evidence to suggest that sharing texts with young children has an impact on later success in school. Maggie Moore, director of Arts and Sciences at Newman College, Birmingham, has spent 17 years teaching primary school pupils, including those with special needs. In an article by Emma Bird on May 2nd 2000, Moore claims she could tell within hours whether or not a child had experience of sharing books with parents.

"Those who had spent lots of time book-sharing had a flying start when entering school because they were confident and enthusiastic - crucial foundations for successful learning. A lot of the time pupils finding learning difficult were not less able - they had simply missed out on the benefits of sharing books, and as a result were less confident."

There is statistical evidence to confirm these theories. The **Book Start** project tracked the development of 300 less priviledged children in Birmingham and found, on completion of the KS1 SATS, that that the children who were given free books and encouraged to read at the start of the study, were approximately 30% ahead in English-based subjects .

As part of the Baby Phonics Method, children are introduced to alphabetic sounds at a very early age. There is much evidence to suggest that children's awareness of sounds is both a predictor of and causally related to their progress in reading and spelling. In a paper entitled "Quality of Learning Recommendation and Rationale", Damon Kerby, Robin Klein, Keli Sato and Robert Vejar stress that phonemic awareness is critical for beginning readers. They quote The National Institute of Child Health and Human Development's (NICHD) report entitled "30 Years of Research: What We Now Know About How Children Learn to Read " (1995), which states "*The best predictor of a future reading difficulty is performance on a combination of measures of phonemic awareness, rapid naming of letters, numbers, and objects, and print awareness.*" Therefore, "*Effective teachers of students offer ... activities including listening to stories; learning and reciting nursery rhymes; hearing rhymed stories and making rhymes; clapping and dancing to syllabic rhythms; identifying letter sounds in words, part of words, and words in sentences.*" These are all skills that are developed early with the Baby Phonics Method.

Equally the Baby Phonics Method encourages children to read quality texts that provide good examples of rhyme and alliteration. Parents are encouraged to read and sing nursery rhymes to their children from the moment their child is born. The reasons for this are very clear. Usha Goswami from the department of Experimental Psychology at Cambridge University, maintains *"Children who are sensitive to rhyme eventually do much better at reading, and children who are taught about rhyme are more successful at reading than those who are not given this training"*

Evidence such as this is particularly compelling when we are told that a common policy in schools to 'set' children can have a decisive impact on their educational achievements. Recent claims made by The Primary School Study, by researchers from the Institute of Education and King's College London, suggest that setting can have a detrimental effect on some children. Although pupils in the top groups can have an 'enhanced educational experience', children who were deemed less bright were less fortunate. They say *"While in theory movement between groups is possible, in practice it is frequently restricted, limiting some children's educational experiences and having adverse long term effects on some of those children who start in the lowest groups."*

The Report on the Expert Panel on Early Reading on Ontario claims that " *The best time for children to start learning to read is when they are very young, usually at the preschool level. In the early years…children gain a definite advantage when they are given opportunities to engage in purposeful oral language and early print activities.*" The Baby Phonics Method attempts to maximise all children's potential by starting their reading journey when they are very young. We firmly believe that this will have a positive impact on their later life and provide them with the necessary skills and expertise to become confident and enthusiastic readers.

1

Printed in Great Britain
by Amazon